THE SPANISH CARD

for

Beginners

The Spanish Card for Beginners
The Little French

Cover by: Blue Dragoon Books

Published by Blue Dragoon Books

Published 2022

THE SPANISH CARD

- The design of the Spanish deck dates from the sixteenth century, and the four sticks represented are the reflection of the four main estates of the Middle Ages. Coins for merchants, cup for clergy, sword for nobles and clubs for serfs.

- The Spanish deck has always been used to read the future. In fact, years ago, the Spanish Deck was only used in Spain. The Tarot was known though, it began to be used later.

- The Spanish deck is a reduced version of the minor arcana of the Tarot. It is a deck or set of forty-eight or forty cards. The most used version is that of forty cards (without eights or nines -what are called the "minor arcana") are added the 10 of each suit (in addition to the knave) and the so-called "major arcana", which are those that, generally, are used for divination.

- The cards are divided into four "families", "pints" or "sticks". The sticks are "coins", "cups", "swords" and "clubs", each of which corresponds to its characteristic iconography.

- The Spanish deck has a series of peculiarities that make it different from the rest of card designs. First of all, they are the only cards that do not have a queen, and as we all know, the figures of the Spanish deck are "Knive" "Horse" and "King".

COINS

money, inheritance
investments, property, luck
the game, the intellectua

When coins mixed with cup
cards indicate emotional an
sentimental stability in the life
the person who consult

If they appear along wit
swords, it announce
impediments or obstacles with
the terrain of possessions an
mone

If these are mixed with club
they indicate that, based o
efforts and purposes, econom
and material stability can b
achieved. Profits or assets ca
also be obtained throug
inheritance

CUPS

love, partner, marriage, happiness, lover, children, family, creativity, friendship, fertility.

When cups appear surrounded by coins, it indicates that we can obtain good security and harmony in the affective or sentimental field in our relationships.

If they are surrounded by swords, it indicates that we have to overcome many difficulties and setbacks to obtain the affective relationships that we have proposed.

If these appear surrounded by clubs, it shows that we will have to work and strive, because it depends only on our own effort to achieve optimal and favorable results or interpretation.

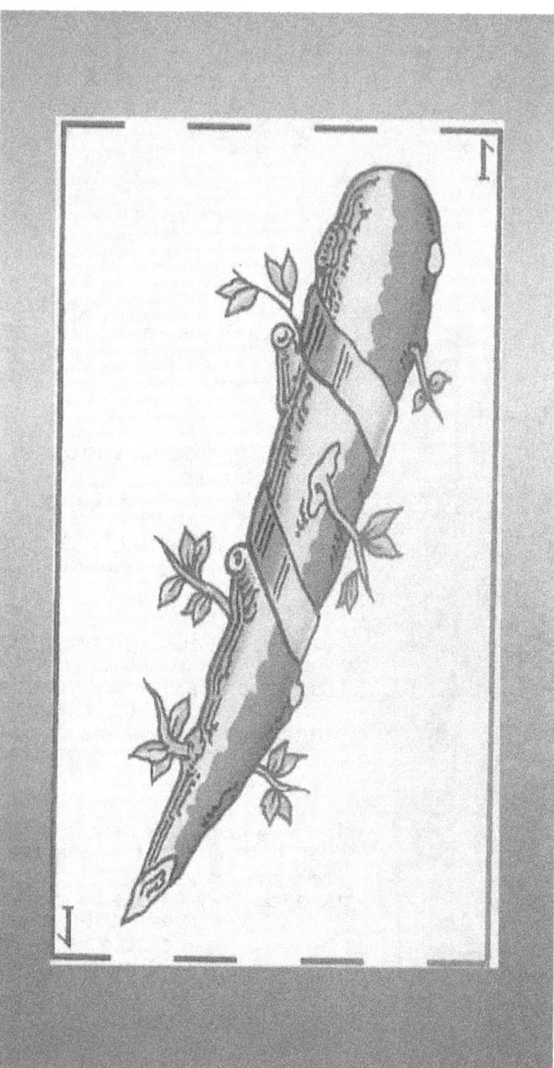

CLUBS

action, travel, travel, energ
work, intelligence, profession
success, project

When they appear surrounde
by cups, it indicates that in th
activity we are doing, we a
going to be surrounded b
people or affectio

If they appear mixed wit
swords, they indicate that w
will have many difficulties whe
it comes to carrying out o
undertaking in any activity tha
we have proposed to ourselve

If these appear with coins,
indicates that we will have goo
chances of obtaining econom
benefits through the activitie
we are doing

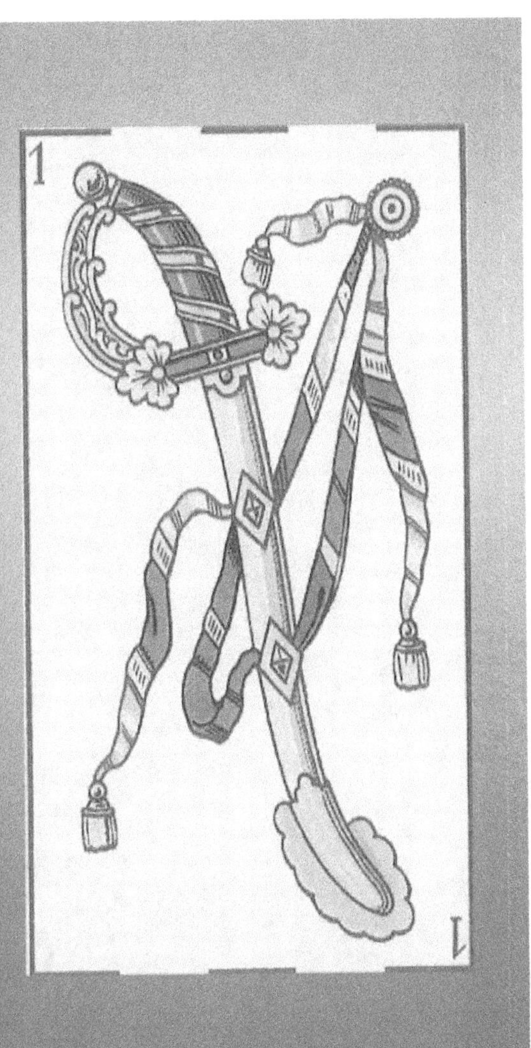

SWORDS

accidents, health, fights, misunderstandings, mood, sadness.

If swords appear surrounded by coins, it means that economic or health problems can be solved.

If they are surrounded by cups, it indicates that all the obstacles or impediments we have in our relationships tend to be restored.

If these appear surrounded by clubs, it announces that our activities tend to improve and increase.

HOW DO YOU OPEN YOUR THIRD-EYE

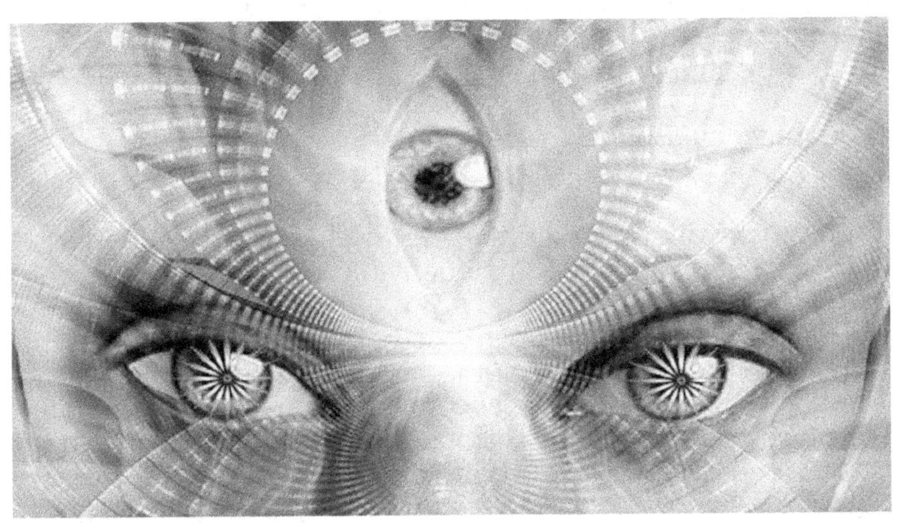

In the brain we have 3 important glands: Pineal, Pituitary and Hypothalamus. The Hypothalamus gland regulates the hormonal part, the pituitary manages the energies of our physical body, and the pineal manages our spiritual field. The pineal is in the middle of the brain, and it is the one that manages the emotional level. If you are charged with many negative emotions, but you are one that channels, you may have that pineal blocked. Blocked... Why? You are going to continue channeling the same, but the filter... an analogy would be: the water filter must be changed because it was covered with soil, so that it must be removed. To unlock it you must release the chakras.

You must work the spine that works, literally, like a **battery**: the occipital bone has a negative charge and the sacral bone has a positive charge. Among them are the vertebrae surrounded by a liquid, the spinal cephalus fluid, which would come to function as the fuses of the body; and that, in case of energy or physical overload (due to some trauma), the fuses deteriorate. **Therefore, it is essential to maintain a good energy flow in the notochord**, so that there are no overloads that translate, for example, into herniated discs or that lower the resources of the physical and energetic body. By freeing it from that layer that forms the negative emotions, the energy flows and thus the chakras open.

The height of the pineal depends on the people. One person can have it higher up another down, how do we test it? Touching little by little, where the third eye is located, and where a small cleft lays is where your pineal gland is located.

The gland for not using becomes smaller, and as we work on it -enlarges, and is very close to the limbic where the emotional level is.

How is it activated?

You are going to imagine a bright white light that comes out forward and backwards from the gland, and exercising and knowing where it is located, it is going to activate. In addition, when it is located with the middle finger, there are two ways to activate it: toning it or soothing it, because it is in 1 of the meridians.

Toning is with small blows - and these should be between 10 and 15 small blows, and appeasing is to rotate the middle finger on top of it counterclockwise.

After this what's going to happen? You will feel like you have a small weight, not pain, but a small weight, like when you are starting to fall asleep, so that you cannot open your eyes because you are very tired, and when you have done the exercises several times, it will start to work, and you will be very connected. A different energy will be handled, and by opening the pineal gland you connect with your Akashic record. And the Akashic record is the library of the universe found on earth, and you are part of that library, you are a shelf.

THE FIGURES

KING OF COINS

It symbolizes a wealthy and sometimes powerful man, self-centered and pragmatic, dominated by material aspects.

It is usually associated with a man with blond hair on the physical plane.

KING OF COUPS

It symbolizes a dreamer, kind, affectious, idealist, weak and bendable.

It is usually associated with a man with brunette hair on the physical plane.

KING OF CLUBS

He represents a voluntary, hardworking somewhat rustic man, with a great sense of duty, dictator.

On the physical plane it is usually associated with a brown person.

KING OF SWORDS

He represents an energetic man, military or judge, somewhat rustic man, symbol of law or morality.

On the physical plane, it is usually associated with a grey-haired man.

HORSE OF COINS

It usually symbolizes the possibility of changing or undertaking any activity related to the material or economic goods of the person who consults.

HORSE OF COUPS

It usually indicates the possibility or attempt of change in the affective field or in the relationships of the consultant. Also, it means activity in this field.

HORSE OF CLUBS

It means the possibilit
of change in activitie
such as work, study,
sports, etc. In some
way, in any activity in
which the consultant i
carried out personally

HORSE OF SWORDS

It symbolizes the possibility of making changes in which adversities and obstacles will be encountered.

KNIVE OF COINS

It symbolizes someone
with an air of greatness,
proud, vain, superficial,
intelligent, selfish.

KNIVE OF COUPS

It represents a loving person, usually young, dreamy, who sometimes does not have his feet on the ground, idealistic and friendly.

KNIVE OF CLUBS

It symbolizes a hardworking, simple, active person, who car have a strict education

KNIVE OF SWORDS

It symbolizes a person who can induce us to make mistakes, who hinders our goals and whose intentions are somewhat doubtful towards us.

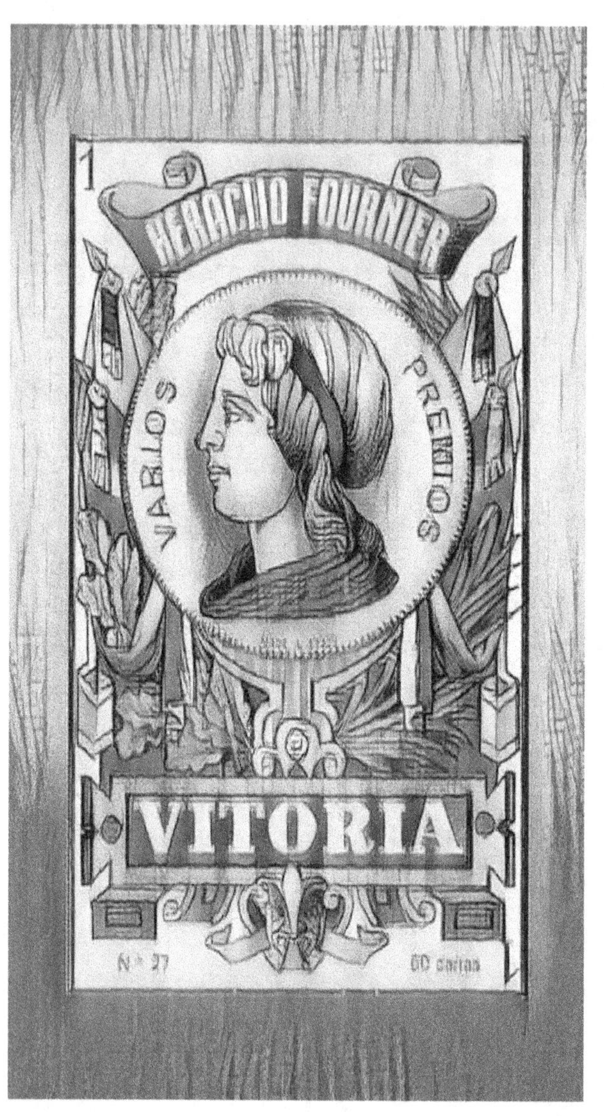

ACE OF COINS

It symbolizes a
success, a union, the
achievement of a goa
or a project.

ACE OF COUPS

It usually symbolizes the home or the environment that surrounds the consultant; it brings some security in the sentimental field.

ACE OF CLUBS

It means the beginning
of something, a birth. It
is a phallic symbol

(referring to
procreation).

ACE OF SWORDS

Generally, it is a card that represents the confirmation of something, ratifies a situation both in the favorable and in the unfavorable.

COMBINATIONS

If coins predominate in an oracle, it indicates that the consultation may be determined mainly by monetary or material issues.

If a greater number of cup cards appears, it shows that the essential reason for the consultation is an affective, friendly or relationship issue.

If club's predominance is enough, it points out that the reason for the consultation is mainly related to labor, study or professional issues.

If the cards that outnumber are swords, this indicates that the person will find serious difficulties and inconveniences to achieve what is proposed.

Ace of sword stick sometimes indicates both physical and psychic illnesses.

Associated with other cards, it will be these that determine to which people or situations they refer.

Three aces

They indicate luck or possibility of success in some issue that arises quickly and unexpectedly.

Ace of clubs with ace of swords

Possible birth.

Ace of Clubs with five clubs

Fight.

Ace of clubs, ace of Swords and Seven Swords

A child who dies at birth or abortion.

Two of wands with seven of swords

Divorce or separation proceedings.

Four of clubs with seven of swords

Possible rape or sexual trauma.

Four of clubs, ace of clubs and a sword

Non-heterosexual sexual relations (homosexuality, bisexuality, etc.) or very unpleasant.

Horse next to seven of swords

Possibility of serious accident or illness of unforeseeable and rapid origin.

Ace of golds next to seven of cups

Possible union, accompanied by sentimental and affective successes.

Ace of golds, ace of cups and seven of coins

Person with possibilities to give an important message in his existence.

Two of coins with four of cups

Fecundity.

Three of coins with three of swords

Love or labor lawsuit.

Ace of Cups with three or five of cups

Marriage.

Ace of Cups with five of swords

Divorce.

Four of cups with (king or knive of any card)

Person with children

Ace of sword with seven of swords

Death.

Four of swords with two of swords

Sick at home.

Seven of swords with four of swords

Serious illness.

THE CARDS

TWO OF GOLDS

Happiness-Short trip.

(Possibility of joy)

THREE OF GOLDS

Surprise-Surprise
Success.

Favorable conditions in
a short time.

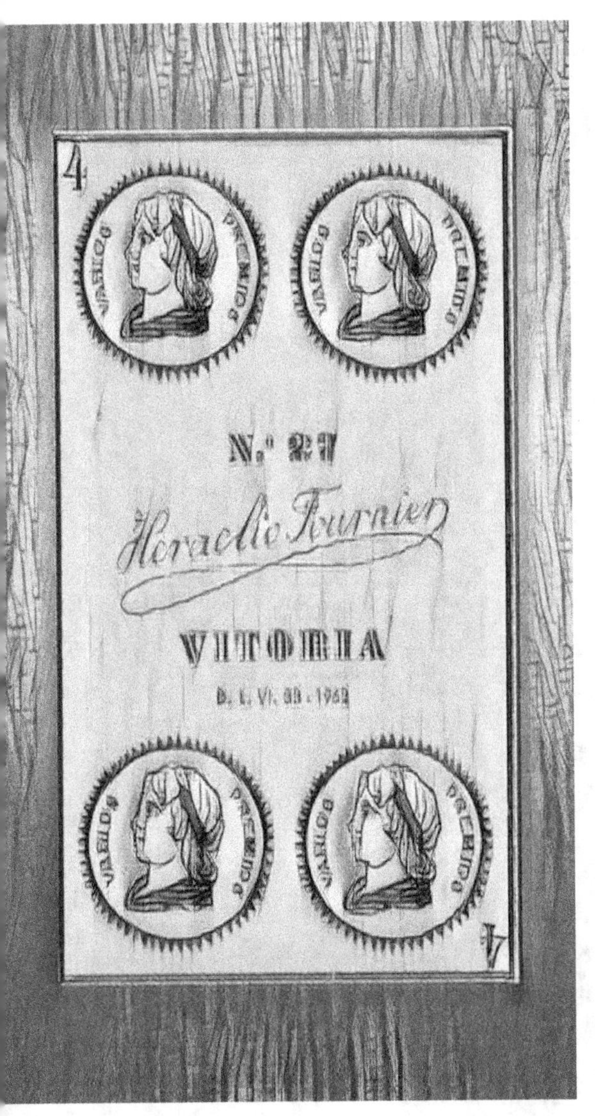

FOUR OF GOLDS

Successful project.

FIVE OF GOLDS

Favorable change.

(But it can also mean losses or slander)

SIX OF GOLDS

Money-Possibility of money.

(Concerns)

SEVEN OF GOLDS

Riches-Joy.

TWO OF CUPS

Good news.

(Unexpected
encounter)

THREE OF COUPS

Abundance-Gift.

FOUR OF COUPS

Joy in Home-Children.

FIVE OF COUPS

Unexpected visit.

(Important meeting)

SIX OF COUPS

Celebrations-Social gatherings.

SEVEN OF COUPS

Dreamos come true.

TWO OF CLUBS

Love bed.

(Person approaching or moving away)

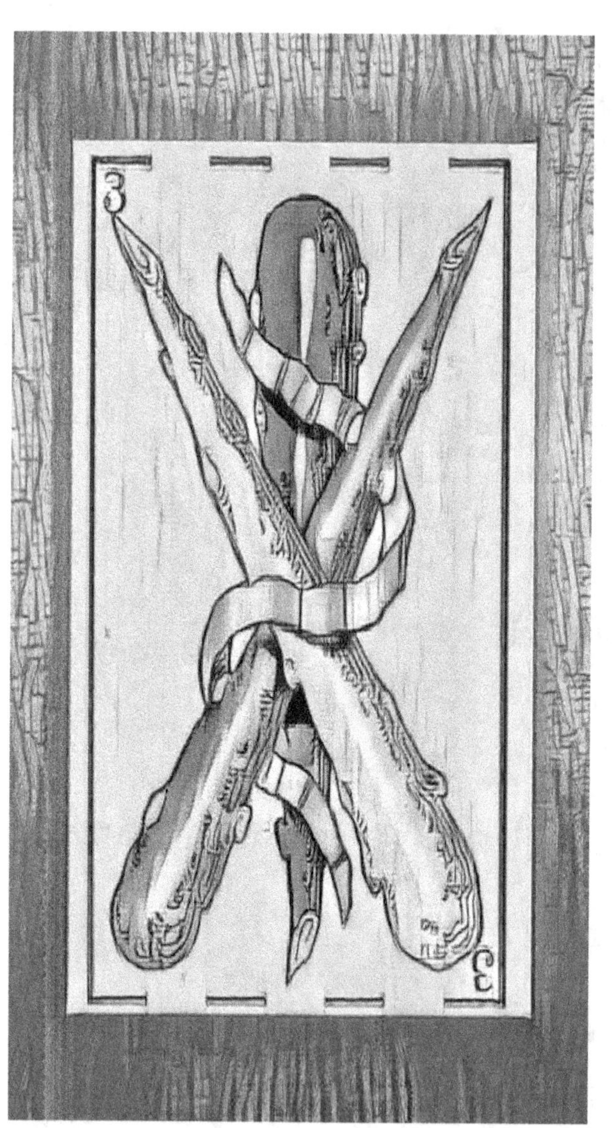

THREE OF CLUBS

Love union.

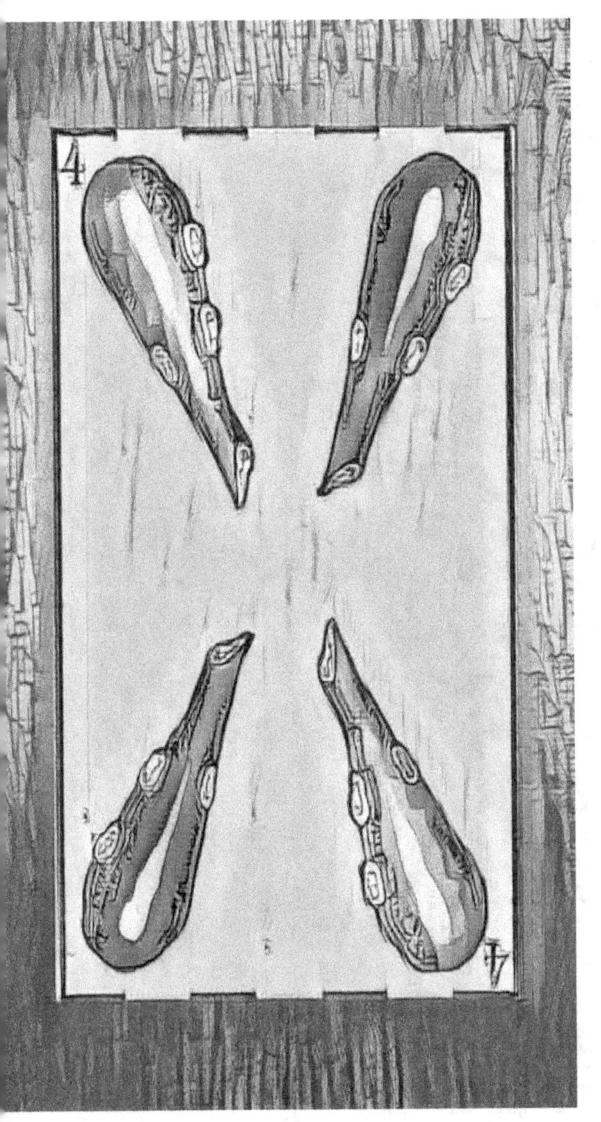

FOUR OF CLUBS

Passion-Purely sexual relationship.

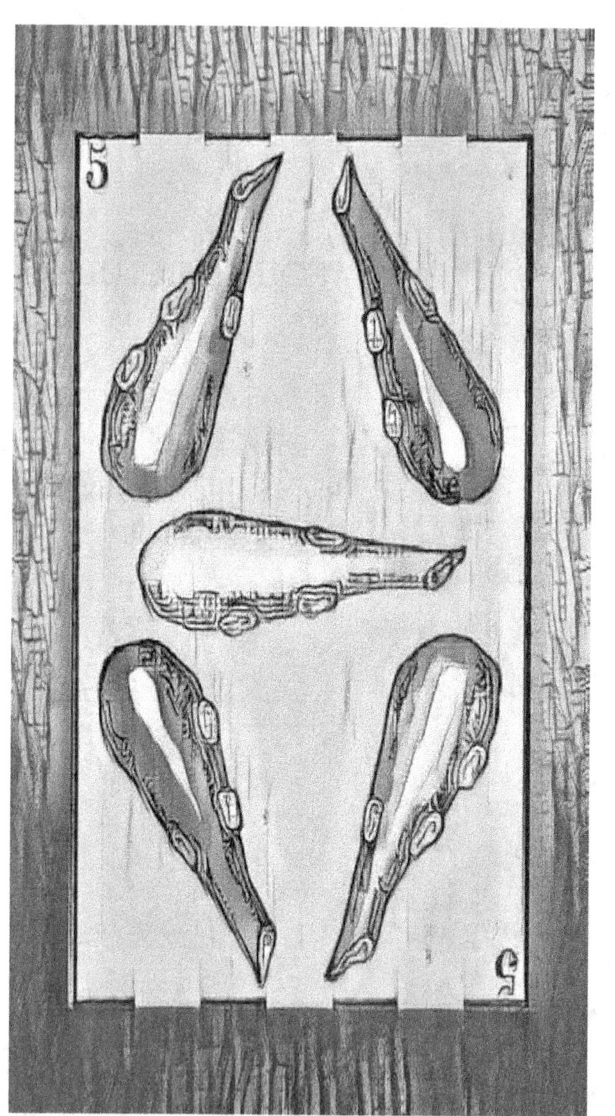

FIVE OF CLUBS

Document-Message o
Interview.

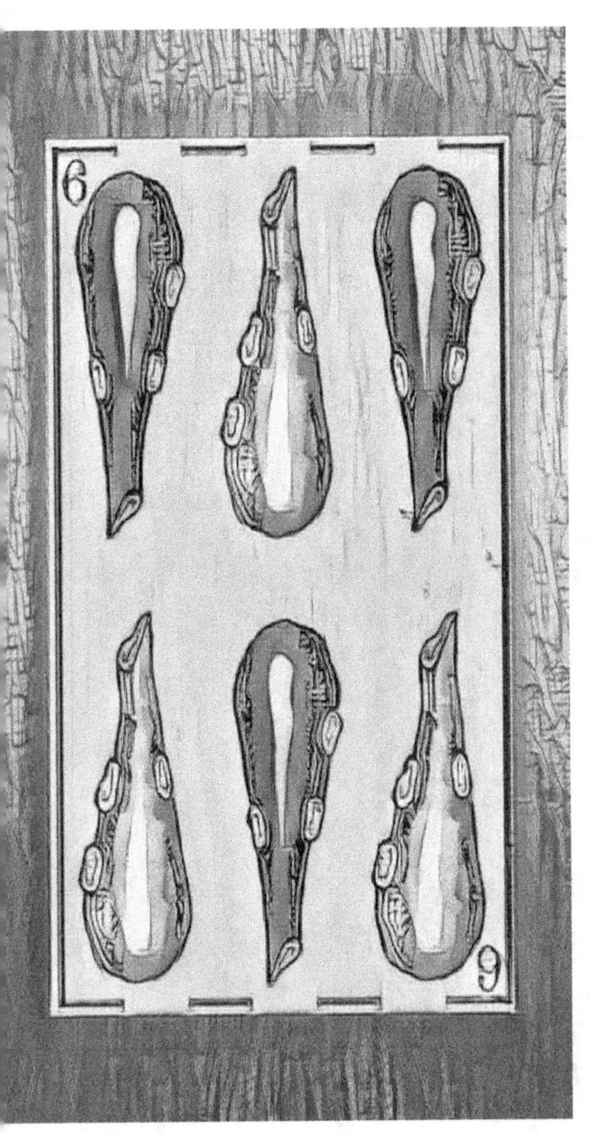

SIX OF CLUBS

Night of love.

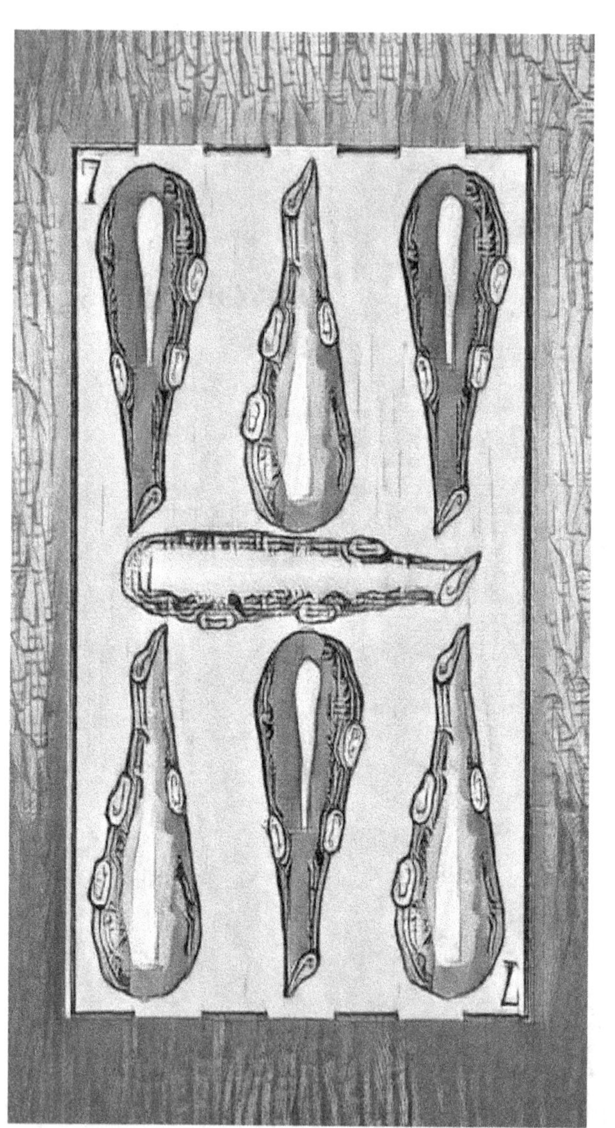

SEVEN OF CLUBS

Sadness-Difficulties.

TWO OF SWORD

Thing that moves away.

THREE OF SWORDS

Setbacks.

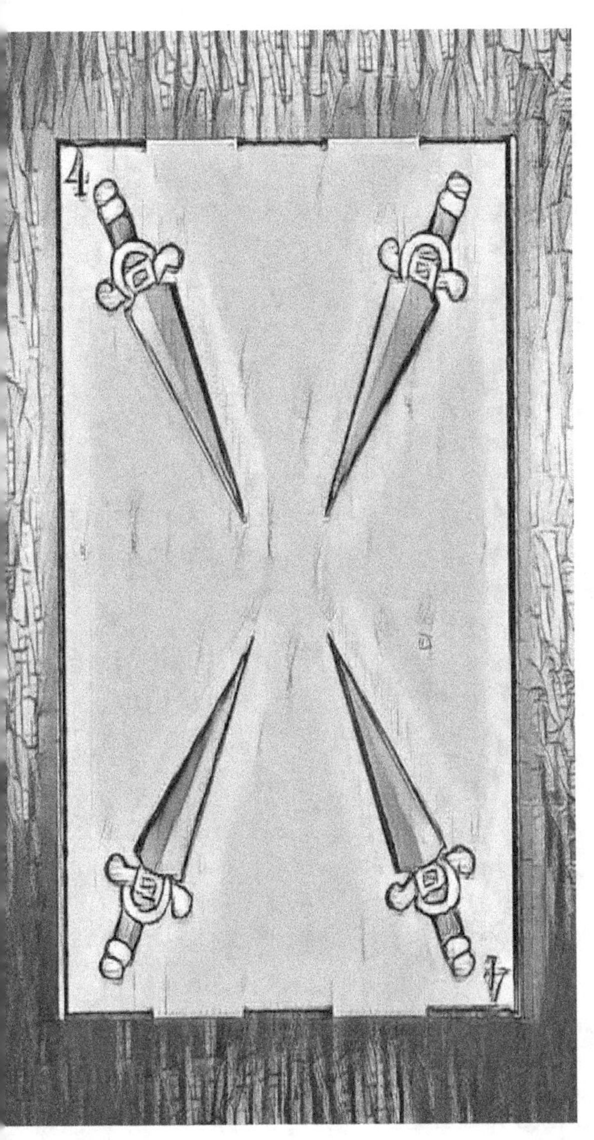

FOUR OF SWORDS

Accident-Illness.

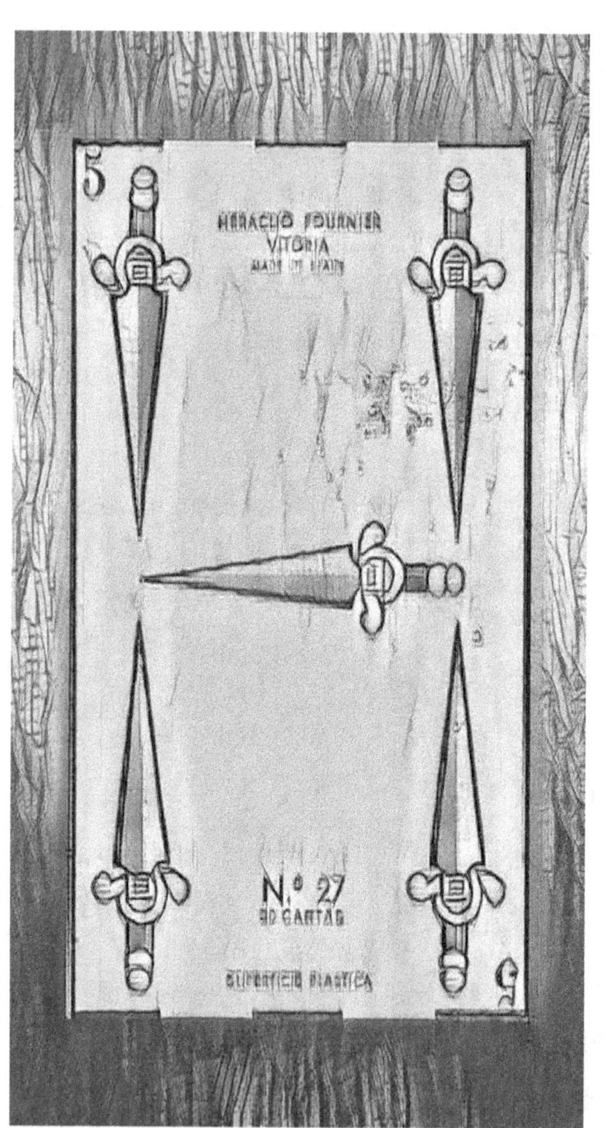

FIVE OF SWORDS

End of something-
Separation.

(Instability and
litigation)

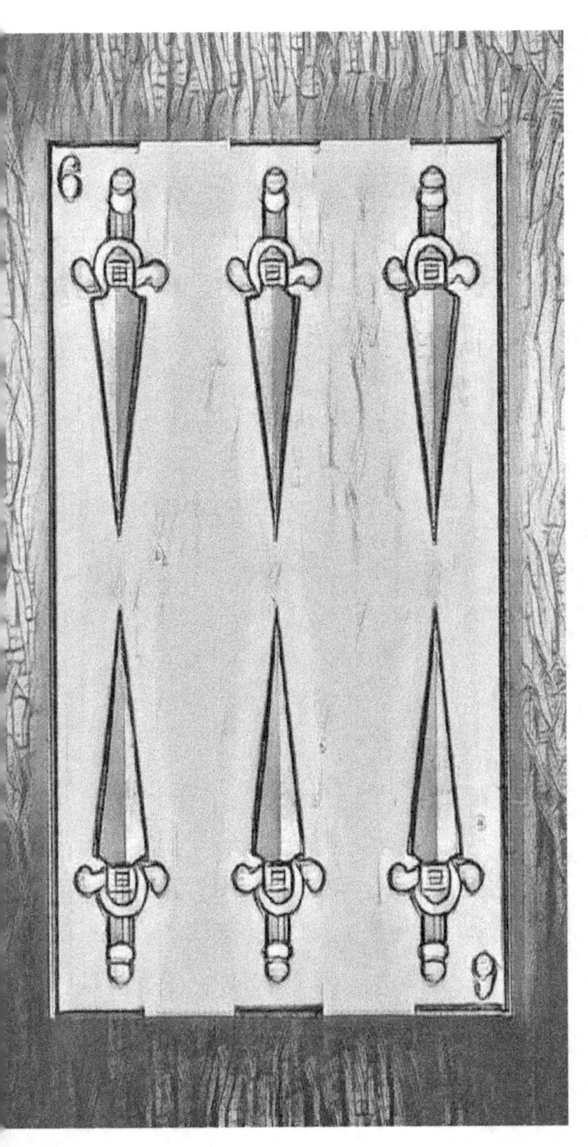

SIX OF SWORDS

Tears or Worry.

(Beginning of
something)

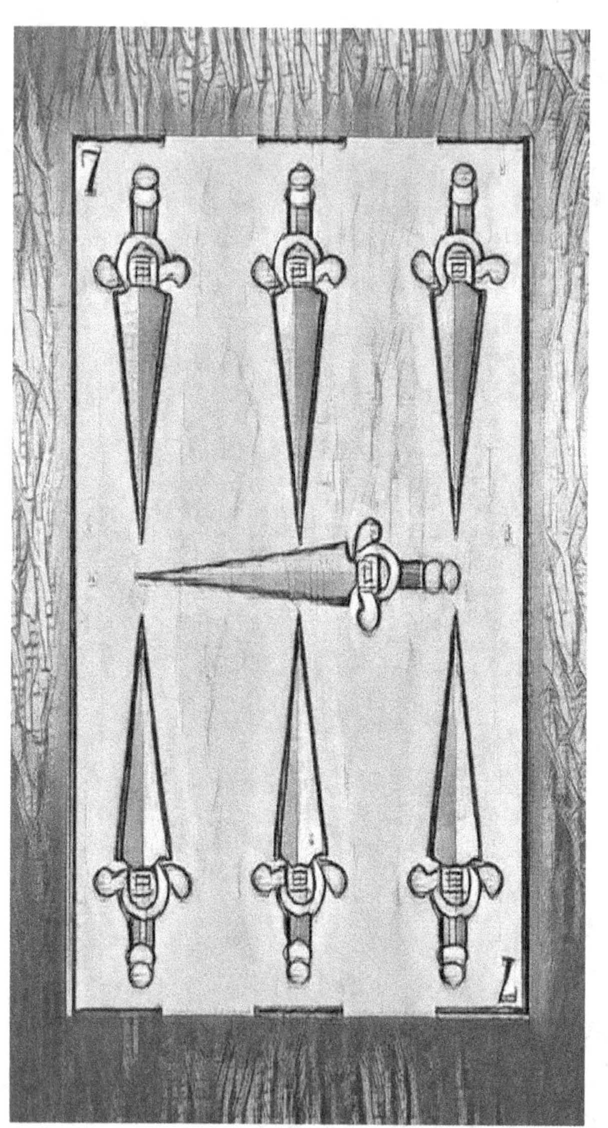

SEVEN OF SWORDS

Telephone call.

THE ORACLE

Before shuffling the letters, you should recite this:

Father: give me the strength to reach my ideal.

Son: guide me to reach my ideal.

Spirit: enlighten me to reach this one.

Mary sheds your rays of light to dispel everything that is not light and help me to discern my Father's message.

Father clarifies my doubts. Father let me know what I need to know. And, above all, let me know what You want me to know.

And if by asking you for this kind of communication between you and me, I offend you; please, forgive me.

- The cards are shuffled twenty- seven times, then they are shuffled seven times again, and it is shuffled three times more and once time again finally.

- Once the preliminary process has begun, the cards are mixed seven times with each other, then shuffled seven times and finally shuffled seven times more.

- They are cut into two decks.

- The first deck that resulted from the cut is put on top of the second.

- The cards are shuffled again and cut into two decks. The first deck that resulted from the cut is put on top of the second.

- And it is shuffled again twenty-one times, and this time the cards are cut into three decks, and the reading is proceeded.

- Each deck for reading is arranged in a horizontal row, and each row must have only five cards.

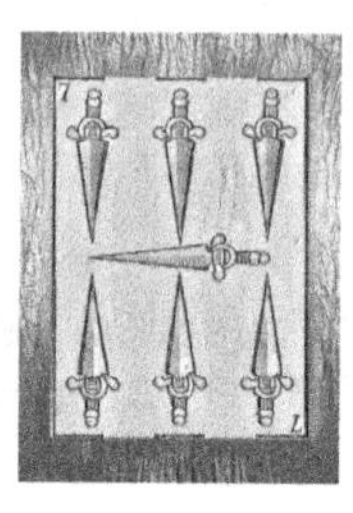

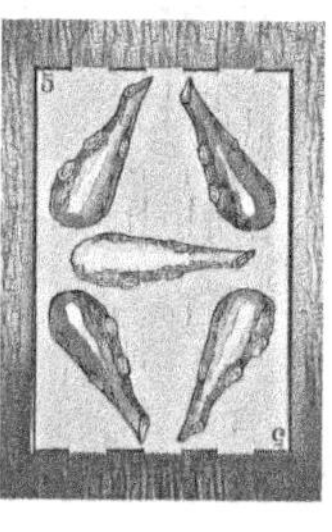

- The cards are shuffled seven times, the cards are mixed seven times with each other, and finally other seven times are shuffled.

- The cards are cut into three decks, and the reading is carried out.

- For final reading, the cards are shuffled again, shuffled seven times, then shuffled three times and finally the cards are mixed only once.

- The cards are cut into five decks, and the consultant must choose one of these. The five decks of cards are arranged as follows:

As you do the exercises of activating the pineal gland – that is: opening your third eye, and in each card reading your intuitive capacity will be activated.

And the practitioner is advised to do meditations.

KNOWLEDGE IS IN YOURSELF....